The Tomorrow Mirror

Nicola Prentis

T0346369

Level 1

Series Editors: Andy Hopkins and Jocelyn Potter

1.1 What's the book about?

Look at the picture on page 1. What do you think? Write answers to the questions.

1 Where is the boy?

....

2 What is he doing?

....

3 What is he thinking?

....

4 Where is he going to go after this?

....

1.2 What happens first?

What do you think? Number the pictures, 1–4.

A

B

C

D

CHAPTER 1

The Bruise

Jason looked at his TV – there was the woman. He
looked in the mirror – there was the man.

O ne Thursday morning, Jason looked in his **mirror**. Then he looked again. Under his eye there was a big, dark **bruise**.

How did it get there? It wasn't there yesterday. Did I do it in my sleep? Jason **thought**. *I didn't fall out of bed.*

He **put** his hand under his eye. It didn't **hurt**. That was **strange** too.

His eye looked very bad. He didn't like it. He didn't want to look strange at school. But Jason was a clever boy.

mirror /ˈmɪrə/ (n) I don't like seeing my face in a *mirror*.
bruise /bruːz/ (n) Children get *bruises* because they often fall down.
thought /θɔːt/ (v, past of think) 'It's late,' I *thought*. 'Time for bed.'
put /pʊt/ (v, past of put) He *put* the book on the table.
hurt /hɜːt/ (v, past of hurt) I'm ill. My head *hurts*.
strange /streɪndʒ/ (adj) There was a *strange* man on the bus. I didn't like him.

'I know! My mother's **makeup**!' he thought.

He went to her room. His mother wasn't there. That was good. He put some light makeup on the bruise. Then he put some dark makeup on too. Now his eye looked OK.

Jason was late for school. He **ran** to the bus stop. His friend Ryan was there.

'Hi,' Ryan said. 'Did you watch the football game?' He didn't ask about the bruise under Jason's eye. The makeup worked!

At school, Jason looked in a mirror, but he **couldn't** see the bruise. His eye didn't hurt and his friends didn't ask about it.

One of his teachers said, 'On Tuesday, you're going to have an important **exam**.'

Jason was a good student. He always did his homework. He wanted to get an 'A' in the exam.

Ryan wasn't a good student. He liked football.

'Who are going to **win** on Sunday?' he asked after school. 'Arsenal

makeup /ˈmeɪkʌp/ (n) Some women put a lot of *makeup* on their face.
ran /ræn/ (v, past of run) She *ran* to school, but she was late.
could /kəd; kʊd/ (v, past of can) I *could* walk at two years old. I *couldn't* swim.
exam /ɪgˈzæm/ (n) In June I have a lot of *exams* at school.
win /wɪn/ (v, past won, n) They're very good at football. They always *win*.

or Liverpool?'

Jason liked Liverpool. 'Liverpool.'

'No, Arsenal!'

'But Arsenal aren't playing well. Are you going home now? We've got a lot of homework.'

'We can do that later. Let's go and play football,' Ryan said.

Jason looked at his books. But it was only four o'clock. Why not?

The boys played with their friends. Jason wasn't good at football, because he was slow. Ryan was very good at it.

The ball came to Jason and **hit** him in the eye. It hurt!

'Sorry,' Ryan said. 'You're going to have a big bruise there later.'

'There was a bruise under my eye this morning.'

Ryan looked at him. 'What are you talking about? You didn't have a bruise this morning. But you're going to have one now!'

Didn't Ryan see it? Jason thought. *Oh, yes – the makeup.* He didn't want to talk about that.

His eye hurt. He stopped playing football and watched his friends. Why didn't the first bruise hurt? It was strange.

hit /hɪt/ (v, past of hit) *Hit* the ball! I can catch it!

After the game, Jason went home. His mother wasn't there. She worked all day, and often in the evenings too, but for little money. There was some food for Jason on the table.

I'm at work.
There's some food for you.
Don't wait for me.
I'm working very late this evening.
Love you, Xx

I'm at work.

He had the food. Then he went to his bedroom and did his homework. Later, he went to the mirror and looked at his eye. There was a dark blue bruise under it.

But Jason didn't want to think about that. There was a **quiz show** on television and Jason loved quiz shows. He moved his chair in front of the TV.

£ 20,000

quiz show /ˈkwɪz ˌʃəʊ/ (n) I love watching *quiz shows* on TV, but I can never answer the questions.

From his chair, Jason could see the TV and the mirror. On the TV a woman won £20,000. There was a big smile on her face. But on the TV in the mirror there was a man, not a woman, and he wasn't happy. The pictures on Jason's TV and on the TV in the mirror were **different**!

Jason looked at his TV – there was the woman. He looked in the mirror – there was the man.

Jason didn't understand. It was very strange. He didn't like it. He didn't want to watch TV and he didn't want to look in the mirror.

I'm only seeing strange things because my eye hurts, he thought.

He opened his school books again. But he couldn't stop thinking about the mirror.

different /ˈdɪfrənt; ˈdɪfərənt/ (adj) My sister is tall and I'm short. We look very *different*. There are *differences* in our faces and hair colours too.

2.1 **Were you right?**

Write these words in the sentences.

bruise	football	hurts	makeup	school	strange

1 One day, Jason sees a .... under his eye.

2 'That's ....,' he thinks. 'How did it get there?'

3 He puts .... on the bruise.

4 He looks at his eye again at ....

5 Later, he plays .... and the ball hits him.

6 Now, for the first time, his eye ....

2.2 **What more did you learn?**

1 Are these sentences about Jason or Ryan – or Jason *and* Ryan?

	Jason	Ryan
a He goes to school on the bus.	✓	◯
b He is a good student.	◯	◯
c He likes Arsenal.	◯	◯
d He is good at football.	◯	◯
e His mother is always working.	◯	◯
f He loves TV quiz shows.	◯	◯

2 Talk about these questions.

a On Thursday evening, what does Jason watch on TV? What does he see?

b What does he see at the same time in his mirror? Why is this strange?

c What does Jason think about the difference?

2.3 Language in use

Look at the sentences on the right.
Then finish these sentences.

'You're **going to** have an important exam.'

'Who's **going to** win on Sunday?'

What are the people thinking or saying?

A Liverpool

.... win.

B You ....
have a big bruise.

C I ....
work late this evening.

D My family and I
....
have a holiday.

2.4 What happens next?

Talk about Jason's room (Picture A). What is different in the mirror (Picture B)?

A

B

CHAPTER 2

The Mirror

Then suddenly, the mirror went dark. Now Jason
was scared. He ran out of his room.

On Friday morning, Jason's eye was blue and green, but he didn't put any makeup on it.

'Look at my eye!' he said to Ryan.

Ryan looked. 'Yes, that's a big black bruise!'

'Black? I looked in the mirror this morning and it was blue and green.'

'No, it's black.'

'You're wrong!' Jason said. *Why did Ryan say that?* he thought.

After school, he went home. His mother was at work again, but there was food for him in the kitchen. He put his school bag on the floor. There was a TV in the kitchen. He wanted to watch the quiz show again.

Today there was a man on the show. It was the same man – the unhappy man from the TV in the mirror.

The first question was: 'In which country is Casablanca?'

'It's in Spain,' the man answered.

No, it isn't, Jason thought. *It's in Morocco.*

Jason's answer was right and the man's was wrong. The man answered five questions and he only won £10. He looked unhappy.

Jason went slowly up to his bedroom and opened the door. There were some books on the floor and some jeans on his chair. He didn't go in. He stayed at the door and looked at the mirror. In the mirror there were books on the floor and jeans on the chair too.

He walked to the mirror and looked at his eye. The bruise was dark blue with some green. But where was his white school shirt? The shirt in the mirror was red! Jason and Mirror Jason were different.

He looked down at the floor in the mirror, and there was his school bag near his bed. But his school bag wasn't in his bedroom. It was in the kitchen!

Then suddenly, the mirror went dark. Now Jason was **scared**.

He ran out of his room. He ran out of the house and into the street. He didn't stop running. He went to Ryan's house and they talked for a long time about the strange mirror.

'Then it went dark,' Jason said.

'What? How can a mirror go dark?'

'I don't know. There was light in my room.'

'Phone your mother. You can sleep here. Tomorrow we're going to go to your house. I want to look in your mirror.'

'Thank you.' Jason was happy about that. 'But aren't you scared?'

'Me? I'm not scared of a mirror!'

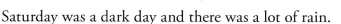

Saturday was a dark day and there was a lot of rain.

'Can I have some jeans and a shirt?' Jason asked Ryan in the morning. 'I don't want to put on my school shirt again.'

'OK. My brother's tall too.'

Ryan went to his brother's room. He came back with some blue jeans and a red shirt.

'Are these OK?' he asked.

The shirt from the mirror! Jason was scared again.

scared /skeəd/ (adj) He doesn't like swimming because he's *scared* of water.

They went to Jason's house.

'Jason!' his mother said. 'What did you do to your eye?'

'It's OK. A football hit me. We're going to do our homework.'

'Good boys,' she said. 'I moved your school bag, Jason. I put it in your room –'

'– near the bed?' Jason said.

'Yes. How did you know?' She looked at Jason strangely.

The boys went up to Jason's room. Ryan went to the mirror, but Jason stayed near the door. He didn't want to look.

'How is this mirror strange?' Ryan said. 'It looks OK.'

Jason went to the mirror. A red shirt. Then he looked at the room in the mirror.

'Look at the floor. Can you see the differences now?' he said.

Ryan looked at the room and then he looked in the mirror again.

'Your bag ...' he said slowly.

'Yes, it's on the *table* in the mirror, not on the floor. And look, my jeans are on the bed, not on the chair.'

'You're right. This mirror *is* strange.'

Suddenly, the room went dark. In the mirror the lights were on. Ryan and Jason were very scared.

Jason ran out of the room. The house was dark. He went to the kitchen.

'Jason?' his mother said. 'It's OK. It's the heavy rain. There's a problem with the lights, but ...'

Suddenly, the lights were on again. '… it's OK now.'

Jason went back to his room. Ryan was at the mirror.

'Why are the room and the mirror different?' Ryan said. Then he smiled. 'Ah! I understand it now.'

Ryan had his phone in his hand. He put it near the mirror.

'Look at the time,' he said.

Jason looked at the time on the phone in the mirror.

'It's 4.10,' he said.

'Yes, the time's the same. Look again.'

Jason looked at the mirror phone. '5 May. But today's 4 May.'

'Yes!' Ryan said. 'The mirror can see tomorrow!'

'You're right! We can watch tomorrow's game today in the mirror!'

'Yes, OK,' Ryan said. He smiled. 'But Arsenal are going to win!'

Jason closed his bedroom door and they watched the game in the mirror.

'Oh no! Liverpool won. You were right,' Ryan said after the game.

On Sunday, Ryan went to Jason's house again. They watched the same football game.

'This mirror can **help** us with our exams,' Ryan said. 'We can win quiz shows or the **lottery**!'

'What? How can it help with exams?'

'We can take it to school tomorrow and we can look at Tuesday's exam questions in the mirror. We're going to get an "A"!'

'I don't want to look.' Jason wasn't happy. 'I often get an "A".'

'But you don't win the lottery. I'm going to take the mirror.'

'No!' Jason said, but Ryan was quick. He put the mirror in his bag.

'You can't stop me!' he said. 'Tomorrow I'm going to look at the exam.'

◆

On Monday, at school, Jason watched Ryan. Ryan had the mirror in his bag. He put the bag near his table and looked into it. Then he moved it and looked again and again. The teacher had his back to the students and didn't see. Only Ryan's friends looked at him strangely.

'Did you see the exam questions?' Jason asked quietly.

'Yes,' Ryan said. 'Now we can think about the answers.'

Jason wasn't happy about that. It was wrong. 'I don't want to know the questions,' he said.

help /help/ (v) Can you *help* me, please? I can't find my bag.
lottery /ˈlɒtəri/ (n) I buy a *lottery* ticket every week, but I never win any money.

3.1 # Were you right?

Look at your answers to Activity 2.4. Then look at sentences 1–6. Which sentences (A–F) come after them?

1 Jason sees the same man on the quiz show. ◯

2 Jason sees the red shirt in the mirror. ◯

3 In the mirror, Jason's bag is near his bed. ◯

4 Jason's bedroom goes dark. ◯

5 Ryan looks at his phone in the mirror. ◯

6 They watch football on the TV in the mirror. ◯

A There's a problem with the lights.   D Liverpool win.

B It says 5 May – tomorrow!   E It's Ryan's brother's.

C He only wins £10.   F His mother put it there.

3.2 # What more did you learn?

Write the words in the sentences.

couldn't   exam   lottery   scared   understand   wrong

What does Jason think?

1 'I'm .... of the mirror.'
2 'Ryan has the mirror. I .... stop him!'
3 'I don't want to know the questions. This is ....'

What does Ryan think?

4 'Now I .... this mirror.'
5 'We can win the .... with the mirror.'
6 'I'm going to look at the .... in the mirror.'

3.3

Language in use

Look at the sentences on the right.

Sentences 1–8 are wrong.
Make them right.

> Jason **watched** Ryan.
>
> Jason **wasn't** happy about that.

1 On Friday morning, Jason ~~put~~ makeup on his eye. ......*didn't put*......

2 That afternoon, he didn't watch the quiz show again. ....

3 His school bag was in his bedroom. ....

4 Jason didn't run out of his room. ....

5 At the weekend, the boys went to school. ....

6 Arsenal won the football game. ....

7 Ryan didn't put the mirror in his bag. ....

8 Jason wanted to know the exam questions. ....

3.4

What happens next?

What do you think? Tick (✔) the right pictures.

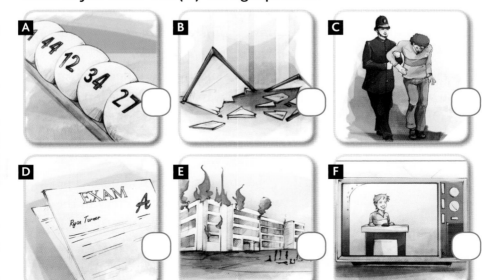

The Fire

Suddenly, there was a lot of noise.
'Fire!' a boy said. People started to run.

Tuesday was the day of the exam. Ryan was happy before and after it. It wasn't very difficult for Jason, because he was a good student.

'I don't like this,' he said. 'It's wrong. I don't want to know about tomorrow. Exams, lottery – it's all wrong.' He was angry. 'It's my mirror. Give it back to me!'

'Why? You can have it tomorrow. I'm going to look at the lottery numbers on TV in the mirror. Tomorrow I'm going to win a lot of money and I'm going to be famous!' Ryan was angry too. He went home and he didn't come back to school in the afternoon.

Jason was unhappy. He wanted to talk to his mother, but she was at work again that evening.

With the lottery money, she can stop working every night. Jason started to think. *Perhaps the lottery is different from an exam. You work for an exam, but you don't work for a lottery win.*

He phoned Ryan. 'Sorry about this morning at school,' he said. 'You were right. But it *is* my mirror. I want to watch the lottery too.'

'Of course!' Ryan was happy. 'Jason, we can buy houses, cars,

holidays. No school, no jobs. Come now and then you can sleep here.'

Jason went to Ryan's house. They watched Wednesday's lottery in the mirror. The numbers were 27 … 34 … 12 … 44 … 11 … 6.

Ryan was very happy. 'We're going to

win tomorrow night! We can buy a ticket after school.' He looked in the mirror. Suddenly, his face went white and he looked scared.

'What's wrong?' Jason asked.

'Look at my face. It's **burnt**!'

Jason looked in the mirror and then he was scared too. The mirror was always right about tomorrow.

On Wednesday, they went to school. The mirror was in Jason's bag and they didn't look in it. Ryan was quiet all morning. He had an 'A' in his exam, but he wasn't happy. Jason had a 'B' and *he* wasn't happy. He couldn't stop thinking about Ryan's face.

Suddenly, there was a lot of noise.

'**Fire**!' a boy said. People started to run.

'Walk! Don't run!' the teacher said.

The students went out of the room. There was a lot of black **smoke**. Jason was scared. He stayed near Ryan.

'I can't see. Where's our teacher?' he said.

'The mirror was right,' Ryan said. 'My face is going to burn!'

Suddenly, Jason stopped walking. He listened at the door of a room.

burn /bɜːn/ (v) The food's *burning*. We can't eat black, *burnt* food!
fire /faɪə/ (n) I like sitting near the *fire* in winter.
smoke /sməʊk/ (n) There was a lot of *smoke* after the fire.

'Listen,' he said. 'There are people in there! Why aren't they coming with us?'

But Ryan only thought of his face in the mirror. He didn't want to stop and he didn't want to listen.

'Let's go,' he said. 'They can come with their teacher. They're going to be OK.'

'Help!' the people in the room said. 'We can't open the door!'

'We can help them,' Jason said.

'No. I'm going. There isn't time.'

'Ryan! Don't go! Help me!' But Ryan didn't listen. He went away.

Jason looked for a chair. It was difficult with the black smoke in his eyes. He hit the door with the chair. It opened! The students came out.

'Thank you! Thank you!' the teacher said. 'Students, stay with me!'

They all went with the teacher. Jason went too. The teacher went slowly – left, then right, then left again.

They walked out of the school. There were a lot of students there – but where was Ryan? Jason looked back at the school and the fire. Ryan was in there! The fire was very big now. Where was he?

Then Ryan came out of the door. His face was black from the

smoke. Jason ran to him. Ryan's face wasn't only black. It was burnt. The mirror was right again.

'Oh, my face hurts! I couldn't find the door. How did you find it?'

'I opened the door to that room and then I came with the teacher.'

'I was burnt because I didn't help,' Ryan said. 'And I didn't help because of the mirror. I was scared. But you helped them and then they helped you.'

'You did the wrong thing because of that mirror,' Jason said. 'But let's find a doctor for you.'

Suddenly, Ryan remembered. 'Our bags are in school. The mirror's in the fire!'

'Perhaps that's good,' Jason said.

'But we have the lottery numbers,' Ryan said.

'No mirror and no lottery,' Jason said. 'The mirror's bad for us, Ryan. Don't you understand? Did the mirror help you today?'

'No,' said Ryan slowly, 'it didn't.' He thought about his face. It hurt. Perhaps Jason was right. 'I know about tomorrow,' he said. He looked back at the fire. 'We're not going to go to school.'

Work with a friend. It is the evening after the fire.

| Student A | You are Jason. Answer your mother's questions. |
| Student B | You are Jason's mother. You want to know about the mirror. Ask questions. |

Where's your bedroom mirror? Why isn't it in your room?

OR

| Student A | You are Ryan. Answer your mother's questions. |
| Student B | You are Ryan's mother. You want to know about the fire. Ask questions. |

How did it start? Why didn't you go with your teacher? How did you burn your face?

Jason helped people in the school fire. Write his story for a newspaper.

Boy helps students in school fire

His school was on fire. What did 16-year-old Jason do? ....

....

....

....

....

....

....

....

....

....

....

....

1 Talk to a friend. What are these people going to do tomorrow?

2 Work with the same friend.

What questions do you want to ask the tomorrow mirror? Talk about it and then write three questions.

a ....

b ....

c ....

What question *don't* you want to ask the mirror?

d ....

3 Talk to different students about your questions. Why do/don't you want answers to them?

Our first/second/third question is: ...

....

We (don't) want to know the answer because ...

....

3   Now think about the days, months and years *after* tomorrow.

   a   What don't these people want to know

      Do *you* want to know? Why (not)?

   b   What don't you want to know? Write three questions.

     1   ....?

     2   ....?

     3   ....?

   c   **Look at your friends' questions. Ask about them.**

     Why don't you want to know? Isn't it interesting?

     Can't it help you?